U.S. Department of the Interior
Office of Inspector General

AUDIT REPORT

Photos by NPS, MMS, and OIG

DOI's HURRICANE REBUILDING EFFORTS

Report No. C-IN-MOA-0006-2007

September 2008

United States Department of the Interior

OFFICE OF INSPECTOR GENERAL
Washington, DC 20240

SEP 3 - 2008

Memorandum

To: P. Lynn Scarlett
           Deputy Secretary

From: Earl E. Devaney
           Inspector General

Subject: Final Audit Report: DOI's Hurricane Rebuilding Efforts
           (Report No. C-IN-MOA-0006-2007)

This final report presents the results of our audit of the Department of the Interior's (DOI or Department) rebuilding efforts in response to damage sustained during the 2005 hurricane season. We focused our efforts on the National Park Service (NPS) and the U.S. Fish and Wildlife Service (FWS) to determine whether they were appropriately spending supplemental funds to repair and rebuild hurricane-damaged assets. This is the second and last of two hurricane-related audits. The first audit reviewed expenditures incurred during the initial disaster response, while this audit focused on the major repair and rebuilding efforts.

DOI's bureaus were greatly impacted by the devastating hurricanes of 2005. DOI sustained significant damage to 12 parks and preserves, 86 refuges, 68 water monitoring gauges, and the Mineral Management Service's Gulf of Mexico Regional Office. As a result, DOI received approximately $283 million in supplemental funding from Congress to address hurricane-related damage to its assets. As of September 30, 2007, DOI had obligated approximately $203 million on hurricane relief, recovery, and rebuilding.

We found that NPS had made poor progress in its rebuilding. At the end of FY 2007, NPS had only obligated or spent 24 percent of its $74 million of supplemental funding. We found many projects were incomplete or had not even been started. Lack of prioritization and coordination could cause NPS to run out of funds before all hurricane damage is fixed. FWS made significantly better progress in its rebuilding effort than NPS. However, we are concerned that FWS lacked adequate documentation supporting decisions it made to rebuild and expand facilities. Our audit did not disclose any instances where NPS or FWS were inappropriately spending hurricane funds on assets not damaged in the 2005 hurricane season.

In response to our draft report, the Department concurred and initiated action on six of our eight draft recommendations. However, FWS disagreed with our findings and recommendations concerning 1) tracking of its hurricane projects, and 2) collection of insurance proceeds on a concessions property. Based on FWS' response and subsequent additional documentation provided to us, we deleted the finding and recommendation concerning tracking of hurricane projects from our final report. However, we continue to recommend that FWS require the concessionaire to collect and remit insurance proceeds on the affected property.

Please provide us with a response to the report by October 8, 2008. The response should provide the information required in Appendix 7. The response should be addressed to:

Mr. Robert Romanyshyn
Assistant Inspector General for Audits
U.S. Department of the Interior
Office of Inspector General
1849 C Street, NW., MS 4428
Washington, DC 20240

The legislation, as amended, creating the Office of Inspector General requires that we report to the U.S. Congress semiannually on all audit reports issued, actions taken to implement our recommendations, and recommendations that have not been implemented.

If you have any comments or questions regarding this draft report, please call me at (202) 208-5512.

cc: Assistant Secretary, Fish and Wildlife and Parks
     Director, Fish and Wildlife Service
     Director, National Park Service
     Director, Office of Budget

Executive Summary

This report presents the results of the second and last of two audits relating to hurricane recovery efforts at Department of the Interior's (DOI or Department) bureaus. During this second audit, the Office of Inspector General (OIG) visited several U.S. Fish and Wildlife Service (FWS) and National Park Service (NPS) areas affected by the hurricanes of 2005 to assess the progress being made in repairing or replacing hurricane-damaged assets.

During our first audit, DOI's 2005 Hurricane Relief Expenditures (C-IN-MOA-0004-2006, March 2007), we found that DOI had effectively managed its 2005 hurricane-related expenditures. Specifically, we determined:

➤ The DOI bureaus had adequate controls in place for procurement of goods and services in emergency situations.

➤ Purchases classified as hurricane-related were related to hurricane response and recovery, and were reasonable and necessary.

➤ Bureaus accounted for hurricane expenditures accurately; however, there were delays in the proper classification of expenses as hurricane-related.

We are concerned that more than two years after the hurricanes, NPS had made poor progress in its rebuilding by the end of FY 2007. NPS had only obligated or spent 24 percent of its $74 million of supplemental funding. We found many projects were incomplete or had not even been started. Lack of prioritization and coordination could cause NPS to run out of funds before all hurricane damage is fixed.

FWS made significantly more progress in its rebuilding effort than NPS. At the end of FY 2007, FWS had spent $145 million of its $162 million (90 percent) in supplemental funding. Our site visits showed extensive work in progress to address hurricane damages. However, we are concerned that FWS lacked adequate documentation supporting decisions it made to rebuild and expand certain facilities.

Our audit did not disclose any instances where FWS or NPS were inappropriately spending hurricane funds on assets not damaged in the 2005 hurricane season.

We provide seven recommendations designed to improve the deficiencies we noted.

TABLE OF CONTENTS

Note: Photos taken by OIG staff during site visits, unless specified in this report.

WHY WE DID THIS AUDIT

In response to the devastation caused primarily by the 2005 hurricanes Katrina, Rita, and Wilma, Congress provided approximately $88 billion to all federal agencies. DOI was allocated approximately $283 million of supplemental funding. This additional funding has generated significant public attention and scrutiny of how the relief effort is being managed and how the funds are being spent.

Due to the high risk of fraud associated with disaster-related expenditures, the Inspector General community has taken steps to provide timely oversight. The President's Council on Integrity and Efficiency (PCIE) coordinated efforts among the agency Inspectors General. Our office participated in this overall PCIE effort by providing information on DOI recovery efforts. Additionally, we planned a series of audits intended to timely review DOI's disaster-related expenditures. Our first audit addressed the appropriateness of expenses incurred during the initial disaster response. This audit addressed the repair and rebuilding of NPS and FWS facilities in the affected areas.

We conducted this audit to determine whether DOI was appropriately spending supplemental funds to repair and rebuild assets damaged in the 2005 hurricane season.

BACKGROUND

NPS Website Photo of Ranger Station Damaged by Hurricane Katrina

The impact of the 2005 Atlantic hurricane season was widespread and devastating. With at least 2,280 deaths and recorded damages of over $100 billion, it was the most active season in recorded history. Some of the greatest impact of the season was felt on the Gulf Coast, where Hurricane Katrina devastated a long stretch of coast along Louisiana, Mississippi, and Alabama.

DOI facilities sustained significant damage during the 2005 hurricane season. DOI's losses included significant damage to 12 NPS parks and preserves, 86 FWS refuges, 68 U.S. Geological Survey (USGS) water monitoring gauges, and the Minerals Management Service's (MMS) Gulf of Mexico regional office building.

We focused on FWS and NPS because these bureaus received the greatest portion, nearly 83 percent, of the supplemental funding awarded to DOI. As of September 2007, NPS and FWS had obligated or spent approximately $162.6 million, or 69 percent, of their $236 million in supplemental appropriations. The breakdown by bureau is summarized in the following table:

Bureau	Supplemental Funding *	Amount Obligated *	Percent Spent
FWS	$162	$145.0	90%
NPS	74	17.6	24%
MMS	31	27.5	89%
USGS	16	12.5	78%
Total	$283	$202.6	72%

* In Millions

RESULTS OF AUDIT

Our audit did not disclose any instances where DOI inappropriately spent hurricane funds on assets not damaged in the 2005 hurricane season. However, we found:

> ➤ NPS made poor progress in rebuilding hurricane-damaged properties because of its complicated and time-consuming project approval process.

> ➤ Lack of prioritization and coordination could cause NPS to run out of funds before all hurricane damage is fixed.

> ➤ FWS made significant progress in rebuilding, but did not adequately document the rebuilding decisions it made.

> ➤ Neither FWS nor NPS were adequately monitoring compliance with construction subcontracting limitations on small business contracts.

> ➤ FWS had not required the collection of hazard insurance proceeds available on a concessioner-operated facility that was damaged by a hurricane.

NPS Made Poor Progress in Rebuilding

We found that NPS made poor progress in its rebuilding efforts and by the end of FY 2007, NPS had only obligated 24 percent, or $17.6 million, of its $74 million appropriation. Nearly two years after the hurricanes struck, we found many projects were incomplete or had not even been started. Following are some examples.

The Loop Road at the Big Cypress National Preserve sustained significant damage from the hurricanes, with a $6.3 million estimated cost to repair it. No progress had been made in repairing this road, and NPS records indicated that this project was not slated to begin until FY 2010.

Damage to Big Cypress Loop Road still not repaired as of our site visit.

Gulf Islands National Seashore

The visitor center at Gulf Islands National Seashore sustained serious damage during Hurricane Katrina. When we visited, the visitor center was still closed, pending the approval to begin repairs. NPS had stabilized the damaged building and was leasing a temporary building until the repairs were completed.

NPS photos of the Visitor Center before Hurricane Katrina, just after Hurricane Katrina, and OIG photo of the visitor center during our site visit.

On West Ship Island (one of the Gulf Islands), every structure was destroyed during the 2005 hurricanes, with the exception of Fort Massachusetts. When we visited, only the boardwalk had been repaired and temporary comfort stations were installed to accommodate visitors.

Red circles highlight structures on West Ship Island that were destroyed, as shown in the middle photo taken after the 2005 hurricanes. Before and after photos are courtesy of NPS. The third photo is an OIG photo of the repaired boardwalk.

Jean Lafitte National Historical Park and Preserve

The historic cemetery at Jean Lafitte National Historical Park and Preserve was badly damaged during the 2005 hurricanes, and grave markers were displaced or destroyed. NPS planned to conserve or repair an estimated 3,400 grave markers and the brick wall surrounding the cemetery. When we visited, the brick wall had been stabilized, but the rebuilding project was still in the pre-planning phase.

Jean Lafitte: OIG photos of the condition of the damaged wall and grave markers during our site visit.

NPS' Complicated Construction Planning and Approval Process Hampers Progress

We believe that NPS' lack of progress may be primarily attributed to its complicated construction planning and approval process. NPS generally uses a 5-year planning and

4

approval process for construction projects. NPS officials told us that any hurricane-related projects totaling more than $500,000 were processed through their standard 5-year construction planning process. This construction planning and approval process involves 49 steps, divided into phases:

- ➤ Planning phase has 9 steps,
- ➤ Pre-design phase has 16 steps,
- ➤ Design phase has 14 steps,
- ➤ Construction phase has 5 steps, and
- ➤ Post-construction phase has 5 steps.

NPS management told us that the process can be accelerated for emergency projects, and cited that in most cases, the planning and design phase for the hurricane projects had been reduced to 1½ years rather than the standard 3 years. Additionally, NPS stated that the standard 5-year planning process had some additional evaluation steps which were not applied to hurricane related projects. However, despite these measures, significant rebuilding had not occurred over two years after the hurricanes. According to NPS officials we talked to, the time consuming process has caused bottlenecks in construction projects and has significantly delayed progress in the rebuilding effort.

After the 2005 hurricanes, NPS identified an immediate need for emergency funds, and Congress responded with two supplemental appropriations. While NPS needs to ensure that it receives the best value for contracted goods and services, some of the delays we noted seem excessive. In our view, NPS is not justifying its need for this emergency funding and is jeopardizing its credibility for future requests by not utilizing these funds in a timely manner.

Lack of Prioritization and Coordination Could Cause NPS to Run Out of Funds Before All Hurricane Damage is Fixed

Southeast Regional Office personnel and a committee of park representatives established a priority listing for all hurricane projects, and identified the top 40 priorities as health and safety related. However, we noted instances where lower priority projects were completed, while higher priority projects remained unfinished. For example, NPS had not completed its top five priority health and safety projects, but had completed several of its lowest priority projects.

We also noted a lack of coordination between the personnel that maintain the priority list and the personnel overseeing project completion. The priority list is maintained in the Southeast Regional Office, but the projects were assigned to the Denver Service Center (DSC) or the parks for planning and design. However, project managers are not accountable for completing projects in order of priority.

This lack of prioritization and coordination could cause NPS to run out of money before all hurricane-related damage is repaired. NPS officials estimate that a project's ultimate cost could be as much as 35 percent higher than the damage estimate currently being used. Based on this estimate, we believe that NPS will not have sufficient funds to complete all hurricane projects. NPS' list of hurricane-related projects totaled approximately $62 million. If projects increase by the estimated 35 percent, NPS will need in excess of $80 million to complete all hurricane projects, which is more than the $74 million in supplemental funding received. Without better coordination and accountability for project prioritizations, NPS is unable to ensure that all significant operational and functional needs will be restored at the affected parks.

> According to NPS records, NPS only completed 8 of the 40 projects that it identified as health and safety issues. In fact, only 2 of the top 10 priorities had been completed as of November 2007. Un-repaired assets included a marina at Gulf Islands National Seashore and an historic house at Jean Lafitte National Historical Park and Preserve.

NPS Malus Beauregard House at Jean Lafitte National Historical Park

Furthermore, NPS did not have a finalized inventory of hurricane projects, and was continuing to add new projects to its approved inventory two years after the occurrence of the storms. In October 2006, the Southeast Regional Office was instructed by the Washington Area Comptroller's Office to allocate $4.5 million for projects in the Gulf Islands National Seashore regardless of the regional priority assigned. This included one project that was not even on the original priority listing. In 2007, five projects totaling $1.3 million were added to the priority list, per the instruction of the Southeast Regional Office Director at that time. Finally, we found that NPS was considering the addition of another $16.3 million project to rebuild the Flamingo Lodge in Everglades National Park to its inventory.

Although the Flamingo Lodge was damaged by the 2005 hurricanes, NPS originally decided not to use hurricane funds to reconstruct the lodge because the building needed to be redesigned before being rebuilt. According to the park's Deputy Superintendent, the concessioner and the park had determined that the existing lodge was not economically viable because revenues did not exceed operating costs. The park acknowledges that it is not economical to simply replace the Flamingo Lodge, and is considering various options to redesign the overnight accommodations at the park.

FLAMINGO LODGE, EVERGLADES NATIONAL PARK

Aerial photo from NPS website, Flamingo Lodge Post-Hurricane Wilma

A project to rebuild the Flamingo Lodge was entered into the hurricane inventory in 2006 as a "placeholder" because of interest in keeping this facility available for visitors. Later, in March 2007 the project was deleted from the list because NPS decided to use line item construction funding to rebuild the lodge. As of August 2007, the project reappeared on the list. When we brought this issue to NPS' attention in November 2007, they asserted that the project had been removed from the hurricane list and that NPS does not intend to use hurricane funds to rebuild the Flamingo Lodge. However, NPS did not notify DOI's budget office of its intent to reallocate funding to other projects. Although this project was included in NPS' original damage estimates, the use of hurricane funding at this time to replace or redesign the lodge would severely hinder NPS' ability to complete other projects for which supplemental funding was received.

FWS Made Significant Progress in Rebuilding, but Did Not Adequately Document the Rebuilding Decisions it Made

We found that FWS made significantly more progress in its rebuilding effort than NPS. At the end of FY 2007, FWS had spent $145 million of its $162 million (90 percent) in supplemental funding. We visited some of the most significantly damaged refuges to assess FWS' progress. At the Mississippi Sandhill Crane National Wildlife Refuge, FWS had finished repairs to its Fontainbleau Nature Trail, bringing it into compliance with handicap accessibility standards. FWS had also nearly completed construction of a new visitor center and office complex at the Mississippi Sandhill Crane National Wildlife Refuge and had substantially completed two refuge residences at the J.N. "Ding" Darling National Wildlife Refuge in Florida.

Mississippi Sandhill Crane National Wildlife Refuge.

Concession Building during our site visit to J.N. "Ding" Darling National Wildlife Refuge

New Employee Housing at J.N. "Ding" Darling National Wildlife Refuge

FWS Southeast Region's Executive Oversight Team Ensured that Progress Was Made

Much of FWS' success in addressing rebuilding needs can be attributed to the creation of the Southeast Region's Executive Oversight Team (EOT) which was responsible for decisionmaking for rebuilding projects. This team consisted of high-level regional personnel from refuges, fisheries, ecological services and budget and administration. The team met weekly to review project and financial status as well as to formalize and oversee the implementation of acquisition plans. The team was supported by the Emergency Recovery Team (ERT) that closely monitored and tracked actual construction progress. The ERT included a senior program manager from the Division of Refuges, as well as contract specialists, engineers, architects, and a safety and health expert.

EOT/ERT members told us that their primary concerns were to ensure that the hurricane funding was quickly allocated to projects and that the projects proceeded in a timely manner. The EOT/ERT moved quickly to identify the significant damage and finalize a listing of projects that required funding. EOT/ERT members acknowledged that the original listing of projects submitted for supplemental funding was based on preliminary information and that the complete list of projects was not finalized until after more detailed inspections and cost estimates could be prepared. With approximately 90 percent of its supplemental funds obligated at the end of FY 2007, FWS was confident that the amount of supplemental funding it received would be sufficient to complete its identified projects.

FWS Lacked Adequate Documentation to Support its Rebuilding Decisions

We found three instances in which FWS did not adequately document its decision to rebuild facilities instead of repair them. In each instance, FWS used hurricane funds to build a larger facility than the damaged one and did not document its justification for expanding the facility. Use of hurricane funds to expand facilities was not allowed under guidance issued by the FWS Director in February and July 2006. In two memorandums, the Director stated: "Funds appropriated for repairing damaged Service facilities are available only to restore land, facilities and equipment to the approximate conditions current at the time of the storm damage. The funds are not available for improvements or upgrades to facilities and equipment." The three instances included (see Appendix 5 for a full discussion of each example):

> The Visitor Center/Headquarters building at Mississippi Sandhill Crane National Wildlife Refuge was being rebuilt at a cost of approximately $2.5 million, increasing in size from 4,000 square feet to 10,455 square feet.

> A concessions building at J.N. "Ding" Darling National Wildlife Refuge was being rebuilt at a cost of approximately $1.8 million, increasing in size from 2,520 square feet to 4,519 square feet.

> Two employee residences at J.N. "Ding" Darling National Wildlife Refuge were being rebuilt at a cost of approximately $1.6 million, increasing their total living space from approximately 2,000 square feet to approximately 4,000 square feet.

Based on the contract cost per square foot for construction, we estimate that FWS spent approximately $2.9 million in hurricane funds to expand these buildings in contradiction of the Director's guidance disallowing improvements or upgrades.

When we discussed this issue with members of the EOT/ERT, they stood by their decisions to rebuild and expand these facilities. In each case, they provided anecdotal evidence supporting their decisions to rebuild and expand the facilities. For example, factors supporting expansion included the desire to replace destroyed buildings with new facilities that met the current needs of the refuge and the desire to deploy standard prototype models for visitor centers and residences.

EOT/ERT members acknowledged that they lacked written documentation and analysis supporting many of their decisions. They stated that the scale of this emergency was unprecedented and that their priority was to get the money allocated and the projects started. In this emergency situation, documentation became less of a priority. While we agree with the EOT/ERT's priorities, we believe that adequately documenting management decisions is necessary to ensure that funds are appropriately spent. EOT/ERT members stated that more recent decisions have been better documented and that they planned to prepare guidance on documentation for future emergencies based on lessons learned from the 2005 hurricanes.

EOT/ERT members also acknowledged that the expansion of facilities was not consistent with the Director's guidance. They agreed that it was generally inappropriate to use supplemental funding for improvements and upgrades, however, they felt that in some cases such use would be justified. For example, it should be acceptable to replace a destroyed building with the current standard prototype, although the prototype may be larger than the original building. They stated that they would seek to develop more thorough guidance for when expansion of facilities would be acceptable in future situations.

Safety of FWS Employees

At the time of our site visits, Mississippi Sand Hill Crane employees were still working in the damaged visitor center/headquarters building and the J.N. "Ding" Darling concessioner was still occupying the damaged concession building. We expressed concern to FWS for their safety given that the damages to both buildings were considered extensive enough to require rebuilding of the facilities. To address our safety concerns, FWS conducted inspections on the buildings subsequent to our site visits and determined them safe for the employees and concessioner to occupy during the construction of the new facilities.

Contract Oversight

FWS and NPS did not have adequate processes to monitor construction subcontracting limitations outlined in their contracts. Further, during our review of NPS, we found an inappropriate contracting action at the DSC.

According to the Federal Acquisition Regulation (FAR), general construction contracts with small businesses under the 8(a) Program must include clause 52.219-14. This clause requires that employees of the 8(a) firm perform at least 15 percent of the cost of the contract, not including the cost of materials. Under the Partnership Agreement with the Small Businesses Administration (SBA), DOI personnel are delegated responsibility for monitoring contractor performance to ensure compliance with the terms of the clause.

NPS and FWS personnel indicated that they did not monitor compliance with this clause because they either did not know how, or believed that SBA was responsible for monitoring ongoing compliance. FWS management stated that it is a known requirement that it must monitor the percentage of performance by the prime contractor (15 percent in the case of general construction) and this monitoring is typically performed at the onset of a contract through review of proposal costs and at various intervals throughout the life of the contract. FWS stated that contract specialists review monthly payrolls to ensure the contractor's employees are working on the job. However, we found:

> No formal policies requiring FWS contracting officials to monitor compliance with this requirement.

> No evidence that FWS contracting officials actually monitored compliance with this requirement. While contracts we reviewed included payrolls from the prime contractor and subcontractors, there was no documentation indicating that FWS

contracting officials reviewed those payrolls to determine compliance with subcontractor limitations.

> ➢ One FWS contract we reviewed contained documentation indicating the primary contractor had not performed any of the work under the contract.

> ➢ A contract specialist and the acting chief of contracting in the Southeast Regional Office for FWS were not aware of any formal policies relating to subcontractor monitoring, and did not believe this monitoring was being performed after the initial contract award.

We discussed this issue with FWS Southeast Region management who indicated that they were now aware of this issue and would develop a formal process for monitoring contractor compliance with this requirement.

We also noted a contracting concern when we conducted our work at NPS. Specifically, for Task Order T200007A005, the DSC inappropriately made a payment to a subcontractor that was not identified in the contract as an approved subcontractor. DSC employees told us that they approved the payment because a contracting specialist at the NPS Southeast Regional Office had represented that the contract had been amended to include that subcontractor. However, this modification had not been made. Additionally, DSC approved the payment to the unauthorized subcontractor at a substantially higher rate than the approved contract rates. Specifically, the subcontractor "project manager" was paid at a rate of $161 per hour when price schedules for other project managers showed that they received an average of $86.42 per hour.

Insurance on Concession Buildings

FWS allows private businesses to operate concessions at wildlife refuges and requires concession owners to maintain property insurance to protect the businesses in the event of natural disasters. However, we found an instance where the FWS did not require a concessioner to collect insurance proceeds on an insured building.

We noted that the concessioner, Tarpon Bay Explorers, at J.N. "Ding" Darling National Wildlife Refuge, was required by FWS to carry real property hazard insurance. In a 2004 hurricane, the concession building was damaged, but Tarpon Bay Explorers did not file a claim against this insurance policy and did not collect proceeds to repair or replace the concession building. Instead, FWS is using supplemental appropriations for the cost of rebuilding the facility.

Even though FWS concessioners are not allowed to own any part of FWS concession facilities, FWS Director's Order No. 139, dated November 7, 2001, requires concessioners to maintain real property insurance. This Order requires all concession contracts include a clause addressing property damage insurance for replacement value of the concession facility. Accordingly, the concession contract for J.N. "Ding" Darling includes two clauses relating to insurance:

D) Property Insurance
In the event of loss, the Concessioner shall use all proceeds of such insurance to repair, rebuild, restore, or replace Concession facilities and/or personal property utilized in the Concessioner's operations under this Contract, as directed by the Contracting Officer. . .

Exhibit H, Insurance Requirements
Hazard Insurance: The Concessioner will be required to provide fire/hazard/wind/flood tidal surge insurance on the Administration building during the term of the contract. The square footage of the building is 2,044 square feet. The name[d] insured parties under the policy shall be the Concessioner and the United States of America.

To date, FWS has not required this concessioner to collect the insurance proceeds. FWS has asserted that the concessioner was only required to carry insurance on its business property. However, we disagree as the FWS Director's Order No. 139 requires insurance on real property. Our legal counsel also determined that collection of the insurance proceeds is appropriate and would be sound financially. Had the concessioner submitted a claim, the proceeds would have been about $153,000.

RECOMMENDATIONS

We recommend:

1. NPS establish a dedicated project management team to oversee and coordinate hurricane-related projects through completion. This team should:

   a. Coordinate rebuilding efforts among relevant divisions including safety, engineering, procurement, and finance divisions to ensure that the highest priority projects are completed first.

   b. Establish a reasonable timeline for completion of all current and future hurricane projects funded by supplemental appropriations.

   NPS' Response to the Recommendation:
   NPS agreed with our recommendation's intent, but suggested that we modify our wording to be "NPS train and prepare a project management team that, in the event of hurricane-related events, will be dedicated to oversee and coordinate hurricane-related projects." NPS stated that it had established a program to manage storm and flood damage recovery, with an immediate emphasis on 2005 hurricane projects. Further, it stated that a multi-disciplinary team is coordinating high priority rebuilding efforts among the parks, Regional Office Divisions, and the Denver Service Center. This team is in the process of formulating a comprehensive timeline for the 2005 hurricane projects.

   IG Analysis of NPS' Response:
   NPS is taking the actions necessary to address this recommendation, as worded.

2. NPS develop and implement policies and procedures that expedite the construction process for projects related to future emergency funding.

   NPS' Response to the Recommendation:
   NPS agreed with our recommendation and stated that it was in the process of analyzing existing policies and procedures for storm damage recovery, and is preparing a draft report for expedited procedures. It further stated that it would evaluate opportunities to expedite construction processes in emergency recovery projects.

   OIG Analysis of NPS' Response:
   NPS is taking the actions necessary to address this recommendation.

3. DOI should work with the bureaus to develop a process that ensures timely reporting of changes to supplemental funding project allocations to DOI's budget office, the Office of Management and Budget, and Congress.

DOI's Response to the Recommendation:
The Office of Budget concurred with our recommendation and will work with the bureaus to develop guidance, as well as a process and procedures on the timely reporting of supplemental funding allocations. The Department will also develop guidance on reporting requirements for reprogramming and scope changes of projects funded through supplemental appropriations.

OIG Analysis of DOI's Response:
The Department is taking the necessary action to address this recommendation.

4. FWS develop and implement policies that require:

   a. A cost-benefit analysis for decisions to rebuild or repair damaged property.

   b. A needs-based analysis to justify expansion or capital improvement of damaged property.

   c. A health and safety survey to ensure that a damaged building is safe for occupancy.

FWS' Response to the Recommendation:
FWS concurred with our recommendation, and agreed to develop and implement policies that addressed these three areas, including new guidance that will identify the reviews to be completed and how resulting decisions should be captured and documented.

OIG Analysis of FWS' Response:
FWS is taking the necessary action to address this recommendation.

5. FWS and NPS develop and implement procedures, including training, for ensuring that contracting officers comply with all applicable requirements under the SBA Partnership Agreement, including monitoring contractor performance.

NPS' Response to the Recommendation:
NPS believes that it is already monitoring contractor performance through processes such as the pre-construction briefing, Davis Bacon Act wage interviews, labor checks and surveillances, submission of weekly payrolls, SF 1413 Statement and Acknowledgment, and Contracting Officer's Representative's on-site presence. It also stated that the Denver Service Center has scheduled training that will cover the Small Business Association Partnership Agreement

and, in particular, monitoring compliance with the "Limitations on Subcontracting" clause.

FWS' Response to the Recommendation:
FWS did not concur with our finding, but did agree that it would be prudent to develop more formal procedures and training material covering the requirements of SBA Partnership Agreement and FAR clause 52.219-14, Limitations on Subcontracting.

OIG Analysis of NPS' and FWS' Response:
As noted in our audit report, we found instances where FWS personnel responsible for the oversight of contracts either did not regularly monitor 8(a) compliance (beyond the initial award) relating to sub-contractors, or believed that SBA was responsible for the monitoring. Further, we found an instance where data in a contracting file indicated that the primary contractor had not completed any of the work on the contract.

We are suggesting that formalized procedures and/or training on those procedures should be performed. Because FWS agrees that formal procedures and training are necessary, and NPS states that it plans to conduct a training course on this issue, we believe that both bureaus are taking the necessary actions to address this recommendation.

6. FWS require the concessioner to collect insurance proceeds for the concession building at J.N. "Ding" Darling National Wildlife Refuge and use those proceeds to rebuild the damaged facility.

FWS' Response to the Recommendation:
FWS did not concur with this recommendation and maintains that these insurance proceeds should not be collected because it would "impose unreasonable cost burdens on any concessioner to provide insurance on a building that FWS considers self-insured." In addition, FWS' response claims that "it was not the intent of the Service to have total facility replacement coverage but, rather to have coverage for the concessioner's equipment investments and personal loss items."

OIG Analysis of FWS' Response:
At the time of the 2005 hurricanes, FWS' policy required that concessionaires carry real property hazard insurance on assets they operated, regardless of ownership. Whether this policy was reasonable or not is the subject of our Recommendation 7. Because insurance was required and the proceeds are available to help reduce the financial impact of rebuilding this asset, we maintain that these proceeds should be collected.

7. FWS re-evaluate its policy requiring concessioners to carry real property hazard insurance.

FWS' Response to the Recommendation:
FWS concurred and is proposing to revise its concession policy to require insurance only on a concessionaire's personal property.

OIG Analysis of FWS' Response:
FWS is taking the necessary action to address this recommendation.

MONETARY IMPACT

Issue	Underpaid Revenues
Insurance proceeds not collected for hurricane damage to insured property.	$153,000
TOTAL	$153,000

SCOPE AND METHODOLOGY

We reviewed efforts related to repairing and rebuilding DOI assets damaged during the 2005 hurricane season. Our fieldwork was conducted from March 2007 through December 2007. Our scope included NPS and FWS. We selected these bureaus because they sustained the greatest damage and received nearly 83 percent of the supplemental funding given by Congress. During the course of our audit fieldwork, we issued six Notices of Potential Findings and Recommendations (NPFR) and considered FWS' and NPS' responses in writing this audit report.

To accomplish our objectives, we:

> Reviewed applicable laws and regulations, including the Federal Acquisition Regulation, departmental regulations, and bureau guidance.

> Reviewed the legislation used to provide the hurricane-relief supplemental funding to determine any compliance requirements.

> Conducted site visits and interviewed staff from DOI and its bureaus.

> Reviewed bureau financial records, asset management systems, prioritization lists, and project management reports to assess the adequacy of the bureau's oversight of hurricane-related repair and rebuilding efforts.

> Reviewed prior audit reports, President's Council on Integrity and Efficiency reports, and various other reports issued by the Department and its bureaus providing suggested improvements for managing the hurricane relief efforts.

> Reviewed the DOI's Strategic Plan for fiscal years 2003-2008, and found that there were no specific goals or measures related to hurricane relief efforts.

Our review of internal controls was limited to management's assessment of damage related to the 2005 hurricanes and the appropriateness of the obligation of supplemental funding to projects identified.

We selected the sites to visit based on the following criteria:

> We attempted to visit a representation of sites from both FWS and NPS.

> We considered the level of damage sustained at each site and attempted to select those sites that received the highest level of damage.

➤ We selected sites reported as having obligated or spent the greatest amount or the least amount of supplemental funding received.

➤ In order to achieve efficient use of our travel budget and resources, we also considered the geographic locations of parks and refuges, and selected refuges and the parks within close proximity of each other.

➤ We also visited J.N. "Ding" Darling National Wildlife Refuge, which was damaged in the 2004 hurricane season, and received funds to repair/rebuild at that time. Although our initial scope only included the 2005 hurricane season, issues at this refuge came to our attention during this audit and we expanded the scope of our audit to include this refuge.

We selected a judgmental sample of contracts to review at each of the sites visited for NPS and FWS. We selected an additional judgmental sample of contracts from FWS' inventory of hurricane-related contracts based on a dollar threshold and other applicable risk factors. NPS did not have an inventory of hurricane-related contracts. We evaluated these contracts to determine if they were allowable within applicable guidelines.

We conducted our audit in accordance with *Government Auditing Standards,* issued by the Comptroller General of the United States.

RELATED REVIEWS

We reviewed audit reports issued by other Federal agencies that address issues related to our audit.

> ➤ In July 2007, the President's Council on Integrity and Efficiency (PCIE) issued the third in a series of reports titled *Oversight of Gulf Coast Hurricane Recovery – A Semiannual Report to Congress*. The focus of the report was identifying the progress made on the transition and recovery from the 2005 hurricanes. Each agency impacted by the hurricanes provided a status of their recovery efforts. Key issues cited include:
>
>> • Hurricane relief efforts were at the 19 month mark.
>>
>> • 1,012 reviews had been conducted and 2,308 investigations had been opened.
>>
>> • Inspectors General had reviewed 775 contracts valued at over $13 billion, and had identified $150 million in questioned costs and $58 million in unsupported costs.
>>
>> • Inspectors General efforts had made the U.S. better poised for future disasters, and had detected and stopped a variety of crimes.
>>
>> • Inspectors General efforts had improved communication and collaboration across all agencies and from the Federal to state and local levels of government.
>
> ➤ In March 2007, we issued a report titled *DOI's 2005 Hurricane Relief Expenditures* (Report No. C-IN-MOA-0004-2006). We found that:
>
>> • The DOI bureaus had adequate controls in place for procurement of goods and services in emergency situations.
>>
>> • Purchases classified as hurricane-related were related to hurricane response and recovery, and were reasonable and necessary.
>>
>> • Bureaus accounted for hurricane expenditures accurately; however, there were delays in the proper classification of expenses as hurricane-related.
>
> ➤ In April 2006, the Government Accountability Office (GAO) issued a report titled *Contract Management: Increased Use of Alaska Native Corporations' Special 8(a)*

Provisions Calls for Tailored Oversight (Report No. GAO-06-399). GAO found that the acquisition agencies reviewed, including the DOI, did not always comply with certain requirements when awarding sole source 8(a) contracts to Alaska Native Corporations. The key requirements addressed were notifying the SBA of contract modifications and monitoring the percent of work that is subcontracted.

➤ In November 2006, the PCIE issued a report titled *Oversight of Gulf Coast Hurricane Recovery – A Semiannual Report to Congress*. The key issues pertaining to procurement were lessons learned by federal agencies in the aftermath of the hurricanes. The report suggested that agencies:

- Use advanced contracts.

- Monitor post-disaster procurement.

- Provide sufficient staff to meet mission requirements.

➤ In November 2005, the GAO issued a report titled *Hurricanes Katrina and Rita Contracting for Response and Recovery Efforts* (Report No. GAO-06-235T). The key issues in this report were that agencies must have:

- Sound acquisition plans.

- Sufficient knowledge to make good business decisions.

- The means to monitor contractor performance and ensure accountability based on a preliminary conclusion to ensure good contracting outcomes.

➤ In November 2005, the GAO issued a study titled *Hurricanes Katrina and Rita: Preliminary Observations on Contracting for Response and Recovery Efforts* (Report No. GAO-06-246T). GAO reported that the acquisition functions at several agencies are on GAO's high-risk list, indicating a vulnerability to fraud, waste, abuse, and mismanagement. Therefore, GAO planned to review contracts supporting hurricane recovery efforts to assess the overall performance of the federal government contracting environment.

Locations Visited/Contacted

Department of the Interior:

Office of Acquisition and Property Management	Washington, D.C.*
Office of the Solicitor	Atlanta, GA*
Office of Budget, Policy Management and Budget	Washington, D.C.*

Minerals Management Service:

Procurement Division	Reston, VA*

U.S. Geological Survey:

Administrative Policy and Services	Reston, VA*

National Park Service:

Gulf Islands National Seashore	Mississippi
Big Cypress National Preserve	Florida
Jean Lafitte National Historical Park and Preserve	Louisiana
Denver Service Center	Denver, CO
Southeast Regional Office	Atlanta, GA
Washington Area Service Office	Washington, DC*
Everglades National Park	Florida*

U.S. Fish and Wildlife Service:

J.N. "Ding" Darling National Wildlife Refuge	Florida
Southwest Louisiana National Wildlife Refuge Complex (Lacassine, Sabine, and Cameron Prairie Refuges)	Louisiana
Mississippi Sandhill Crane National Wildlife Refuge	Mississippi
Visitor Services	Arlington, VA*
Office of Information Management	Arlington, VA*
Division of Engineering	Arlington, VA*
Division of Budget	Arlington, VA*
Region 6 Financial Division	Lakewood, CO
Southeast Regional Office - Region 4	Atlanta, GA
Southwest Regional Office - Region 2	Albuquerque, NM*

Contacted via telephone

EXPANDED FWS FACILITIES

Mississippi Sandhill Crane Visitor Center and Headquarters Building

FWS is rebuilding this facility with hurricane funds at a cost of approximately $2.5 million, rather than make repairs. We found that the EOT did not adequately document its decisions to 1) rebuild rather than repair the facility and 2) expand the facility from 4,000 square feet to 10,455 square feet.

During our site visit to the Mississippi Sandhill Crane National Wildlife Refuge, we toured the damaged facility.   Refuge staff showed us that a portion of the roof was sagging and another portion of the roof had been temporarily covered by a tarp. Refuge staff said that the region had decided that it was more cost effective to rebuild the facility, at a cost of approximately $2.5 million, rather than make repairs. However, the existing existing estimate to repair the facility was $945,076. We found no written documentation supporting the decision to rebuild rather than repair the facility.

When we discussed this facility with members of the EOT, they stood by their decisions to rebuild and expand this facility. They stated that in the long run, it was a better business decision to build a new building than to invest almost $1 million repairing an older building without substantially increasing its anticipated useful life. Concerning the expansion, EOT members stated that they chose to utilize standard prototype plans developed for these facilities. There are three standard prototypes (small, medium, large) based on factors such as visitation levels. The EOT chose the medium sized prototype (10,655 square feet) for the replacement building rather than the small prototype (6,400 square feet) which would still have been larger then the original 4,000 square foot building. The EOT members stated that they chose the medium prototype based on their understanding of the needs of the refuge. However, there was no formal documented analysis of needs performed at the time to support their decision. Based on the contract cost per square foot for this building, we estimate that FWS spent $1.6 million to expand this building.

J.N. "Ding" Darling National Wildlife Refuge, Concession Building

FWS is rebuilding this facility with hurricane funds at a cost of approximately $1.8 million, rather than make repairs. We found that the EOT did not adequately document its decisions to 1) rebuild rather than repair the facility and 2) expand the facility from 2,520 square feet to 4,519 square feet.

During our site visit to the J.N. "Ding" Darling National Wildlife Refuge, we toured the concession building damaged by a 2004 hurricane. According to refuge managers, FWS evaluated the possibility of repairing concession retail space and living quarters, but decided to replace the damaged building. FWS did not provide an estimate of the cost to repair the facility and bring it into compliance with current building codes. The new building will be 2,000 square feet or 80 percent larger.

When we discussed this facility with members of the EOT, they stood by their decisions to rebuild and expand this facility. They indicated that the facility was significantly damaged, requiring replacement. Concerning the expansion, EOT members stated that the new building actually replaced two damaged facilities: 1) the original concession facility and 2) a 2,405 square foot "pole shed" that the concessioner had used for storage of equipment. Therefore, the EOT considered the new facility to be comparable to the two facilities it replaced; 4,519 square feet for the new structure versus 4,975 square feet for existing two structures. We disagree with this conclusion. The new building is elevated and the storage area will now be underneath the building. That storage space is in addition to the 4,519 square feet of finished space in the new building. The EOT members also stated that the existing building did not meet the current needs of the operators – thus requiring the expansion. The EOT was unable to provide us with any written documentation supporting their decisions. Based on the contract cost per square foot for this building, we estimate that FWS spent $810,355 to expand this building.

J.N. "Ding" Darling National Wildlife Refuge, Law Enforcement and Refuge Manager Residences

FWS is rebuilding these residences with hurricane funds at a cost of approximately $1.6 million. We found that the EOT did not adequately document its decisions to 1) rebuild rather than repair the residences and 2) expand the residences from 2,000 square feet to 4,000 square feet of total living space.

During our site visit to the J.N. "Ding" Darling National Wildlife Refuge, we toured the residences for the Chief Law Enforcement Officer and the Refuge Manager that are currently under construction. According to refuge personnel, the previous residences were damaged in a 2004 hurricane and subsequently demolished. FWS did not provide an estimate of the cost to repair the residences and bring them into compliance with current building codes.

When we discussed the residences with members of the EOT, they stood by the decisions to rebuild and expand these residences. They indicated that the original houses had significant damage, including extensive mold and that it was a better decision to rebuild the houses and elevate them to prevent damage from future storms. Additionally, the Southeast region had developed prototypical models for employee housing to standardize housing amongst the refuges and to eliminate the time and cost associated with developing unique designs. The decision was made to replace these residences with the standard models, which were bigger and more appropriate for a family of four. Based on the contract cost per square foot for this project, it appears that FWS spent about $480,000 to expand these buildings.

AUDITEE COMMENTS AND OIG RESPONSE

The following table summarizes the comments to the draft report that we received from FWS, NPS, and DOI, and our response:

COMMENTS FROM FWS	OIG RESPONSE
Project Management FWS maintained that it did have adequate processes for tracking and accounting for hurricane rebuilding projects.	We conducted additional work at FWS Southeast Region and were provided with additional documentation concerning its tracking and accounting for hurricane rebuilding projects. We eliminated the finding and related draft recommendation from the final report.
Justification for Rebuilding and Expanding FWS disagreed with our finding related to inadequate justification for rebuilding and expanding certain assets with hurricane funding. It maintained that all decisions to replace facilities rather than repair them were based on sound judgment, good repair estimates, and the best professional opinions of various employees. It also noted that many damaged facilities had to be replaced in order to bring them up to current building codes and requirements. Finally, FWS acknowledged the need to ensure the health and safety of its employees continuing to work in structures damaged enough to need replacement.	We changed the finding to highlight our overall concern that FWS did not adequately document the decisions it made to rebuild and expand some of its facilities. We updated our report to provide more detail on the instances that we questioned – including FWS' anecdotal reasons for making decisions to rebuild rather than repair and/or decisions to expand the size of facilities. While FWS' decisions to rebuild or expand may be prudent, it did not adequately conduct analyses and document those decisions. Additionally, the decision to expand certain facilities were in direct contradiction to Director guidance prohibiting the improvement or upgrade of facilities. FWS agreed with our recommendations relating to documenting decisions to rebuild and expand facilities. Subsequent to our draft report FWS conducted inspections on damaged buildings that were still occupied and deemed them to be safe for employees to occupy.
Contract Oversight FWS believed that it had adequate processes in place to oversee contract issues relating to 8(a) small businesses, but agreed that it would be prudent to develop and implement more formal procedures for ensuring that contracting officers comply with these requirements.	We stand by our conclusion that FWS was not monitoring contractor compliance with subcontractor limitations. We found no formal procedures requiring contracting personnel to monitor compliance and no evidence in the contracting files that such monitoring was being performed.

	Additionally, two FWS contracting employees we interviewed during the course of our audit work stated that they did not know how to monitor this compliance. We believe that procedures need to be developed and training in this area needs to be performed.
Insurance FWS agreed that its concession contract required the concessioner to maintain property and hazard insurance and that the concessioner complied with the requirement. However, FWS disagreed that the proceeds available from that policy should be collected based on the concept that the government is a "self-insurer."	FWS' policy requiring concessioners to have hazard insurance placed a burden on concessioners to obtain and pay for these policies that FWS never intended for them to collect. However, because the insurance policy was in place at the time of the hurricanes and we have confirmed that proceeds in the amount of $153,000 are available, we maintain that these proceeds should be collected and used to reduce the taxpayer burden for rebuilding this facility.
Wasted Funds FWS disagreed with the heading "Wasted Funds" on the table of monetary impacts and asked that we change the title to more closely reflect the issues we noted in our audit report.	We deleted the category of "Wasted Funds." After our visit to to the FWS Southeast Region, we determined that the rebuilding and expansion of hurricane damaged structures may have been appropriate but this could not be evaluated because FWS did not create adequate support for their decisions to rebuild and expand.
COMMENTS FROM NPS	**OIG RESPONSE**
NPS Rebuilding Progress NPS clarified some issues relating to its planning and approval process. For example, it had generally reduced the planning and design phase to 1½ years instead of the standard 3 years and had not applied some of the additional evaluation steps included in the standard 5 year process. NPS provided some updated information on projects that we highlighted in our report. This updated information included several contract awards and the actions it had already taken or planned to take to address our audit recommendations. For example: • Its list of top priority projects has increased from 40 to 43. As of April 2008, 22 of those 43 projects had been completed and 18 were in progress. • Construction for the Big Loop road in Big Cypress is now scheduled for January	We amended our final report to address the additional information provided by NPS concerning its construction approval process – however, we remain concerned that rebuilding progress has been slow.

2009.	
• The construction for the West Ship Island is now expected to be completed by June 2009.	
• A construction contract for the Jean Lafitte National Historical Park and Preserve is scheduled for issuance in September 2008.	
Contract Oversight NPS also stated that it could not find any instances where an 8(a) prime contractor did not perform the required minimum amount of work. NPS also stated that it could not respond to the inappropriate contract action at the DSC or to the inappropriate procurement and payment of a project manager that we detailed in our report, without further details.	We did not find any specific instances of non-compliance during our work at NPS. However, because NPS contracting personnel indicated that they were not aware of this requirement, we believe that training on this issue may be appropriate. These issues are one in the same. The inappropriate contracting action involved a payment to a subcontractor that was not included on the contract's list of approved subcontractors. We amended the report to provide more detail on the issue and OIG personnel provided NPS staff with additional information necessary to research this issue.
COMMENTS FROM DOI	OIG RESPONSE
In its response, DOI agreed to work with the bureaus to develop guidance, processes, and procedures to more timely report the status of supplemental funding allocations. It further stated that developing these processes and procedures will enable DOI to provide more timely reports and updates to OMB and Congress on any changes in funding.	We agree that the bureaus need to have processes in place to timely notify the DOI when they materially modify projects and/or project funding allocations for which they received funding to complete specified projects.

STATUS OF AUDIT RECOMMENDATIONS

RECOMMENDATION	STATUS	ACTION REQUIRED
1	Management concurred with recommendation; additional information is needed.	NPS should provide the name and title of the official responsible for completing the corrective action and a planned completion date.
2	Management concurred with recommendation; additional information is needed.	NPS should provide the name and title of the official responsible for completing the corrective action and a planned completion date.
3	Management concurred with recommendation; additional information is needed.	DOI should provide the name and title of the official responsible for completing the corrective action and a planned completion date.
4	Management concurred with recommendation; additional information is needed.	FWS should provide the name and title of the official responsible for completing the corrective action and a planned completion date.
5	Management concurred with recommendation; additional information is needed.	FWS and NPS should provide the name and title of the official responsible for completing the corrective action and a planned completion date.
6	Unresolved.	FWS should reconsider the recommendation and provide a response that indicates concurrence and/or nonconcurrence and provide estimated target date and the name and title of the official responsible for implementation.
7	Management concurred with recommendation; additional information is needed.	FWS should provide the name and title of the official responsible for completing the corrective action and a planned completion date.

Report Fraud, Waste, Abuse And Mismanagement

Fraud, waste, and abuse in government concerns everyone: Office of Inspector General staff, Departmental employees, and the general public. We actively solicit allegations of any inefficient and wasteful practices, fraud, and abuse related to Departmental or Insular area programs and operations. You can report allegations to us in several ways.

By Mail:	U.S. Department of the Interior Office of Inspector General Mail Stop 4428 MIB 1849 C Street, NW Washington, D.C. 20240
By Phone:	24-Hour Toll Free 800-424-5081 Washington Metro Area 703-487-5435
By Fax:	703-487-5402
By Internet:	www.doioig.gov

Revised 06/08